AZTECS
AND INCAS

Chloë Sayer

ALADDIN / WATTS
London • Sydney

How to use this book

The key below shows how the subjects in this book are divided up. It includes information on Aztec and Inca language and literature, science and maths, history, geography and the Arts.

Introduction

The Aztecs and the Incas were two of the greatest societies the world has ever known. Both ruled over huge areas and a large number of people. At its greatest, the Inca Empire covered Peru, Ecuador, Bolivia and the neighbouring areas of Chile and Argentina. The Aztecs and their allies ruled most of present-day Mexico. Today we can see the remains of these amazing empires.

Created and produced by
Aladdin Books Ltd
PO Box 53987
London SW15 2SF

Design   Omnipress Limited, UK

Designer   Vivian Foster

Ilustrators   Sergio Momo, David Burroughs, David Russell

First published in 2009
by Franklin Watts
338 Euston Road, London NW1 3BH

Franklin Watts Australia
Level 17/207 Kent Street, Sydney, NSW 2000

Franklin Watts is a division of Hachette Children's Books, an Hachette UK company
www.hachette.co.uk

ISBN 978 0 7496 8653 6

A CIP catalogue record for this book is available from the British Library
Dewey classification: 972'.018

Printed in Malaysia

The author, Chloë Sayer, has written numerous books on Mexico. She has worked as a television consultant on documentaries about Mexico, Peru and Spain for the BBC and Channel 4, and has made ethnographic collections for the British Museum in Mexico and Belize.

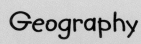

Geography

The symbol of the planet Earth shows where geographical facts are used. These sections look at the migration of early hunters across the Bering Strait, and the natural environments of Mexico and Peru.

Language and literature

Where you see an open book, you will learn about language. These sections discuss the manuscripts of the Aztecs and storytelling among the Incas. They also explore the legend of El Dorado.

Science and maths

Where science and maths are mentioned you will see the symbol of a microscope. These sections study foodstuffs and weaponry used by the Aztecs, and the Inca calendar, quipu and animal husbandry.

History

The scroll and the hourglass indicate that historical facts are included. These sections explore the rise and fall of civilisations before the Aztecs and Incas. They also discuss the arrival from Spain of Cortés and Pizarro.

Social history

The symbol of the family is used wherever information on social history is included. These sections give an insight into the everyday lives of the Aztecs and Incas and the social structure of their cities.

Arts, crafts and music

This symbol indicates information on arts, crafts or music. These sections talk about gold and feather working, painting, weaving and influences on 20th-century artists, such as Diego Rivera.

Contents

Early America

The first people to inhabit the Americas came from Eastern Asia. They gathered wild plants for food, wore animal skins and made arrow heads out of sharp flakes of stone.

They hunted mammoths, mastodons, antelopes, horses and other animals. Later they learned how to make simple nets, baskets, mats and rope. Over a long period of time, separate cultures, such as the Olmecs and Nazca, formed in North and South America.

Before the Aztecs

The first major civilisation in Mexico was the Olmecs, who lived on the tropical lowlands of the Gulf Coast between 1200 and 600 BC. During the 10th and 11th centuries AD, much of Mexico was dominated by the warlike Toltecs. Soon other distinctive cultures developed, like the Zapotecs and later the Mixtecs. The Maya excelled as architects, painters and sculptors.

The city of Copán

After the Ice Age, the changing climate and overhunting killed off several American animal species including the mammoth and the horse. About 7,000 years ago, hunter-gatherers learned how to cultivate food like maize and beans, which allowed people to live in large settlements. The city of Copán was one of the many cities built by the ancient Maya. The city was built with many stone temples, palaces and ball courts.

NORTH AMERICA

Totonacs
Toltecs
Olmecs
Maya
Mixtecs
Copán

Pre-Aztec civilisations

North America

Atlantic Ocean

Pacific Ocean

N
W — E
S

South America

People of South America

The Incas were the last in a long line of important civilisations in South America. These included the Vicús, the Cajamarca, the Nazca, the Tiahuanaco, the Mochica and later the Chimú. The Chimú capital – Chan Chan (right) – was built from sun-dried mud bricks and at one time was home to more than 50,000 people.

Olmec stone head

SOUTH AMERICA

Mochica pottery

Pre-Inca civilisations

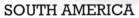

Vicús
Mochica
Cajamarca
Recuay
Lima
Huarpa
Waru
Nazca
Tiahuanaco
Atacameno

The land bridge

During the Great Ice Age, ice sheets formed and exposed a wide platform of land across the Bering Strait, between Siberia and the western coast of Alaska. Between 30,000 and 8,000 BC, many nomadic tribes from Asia crossed this bridge and then went on to live in North, Central and South America. These people lived off the animals and plants that thrived on these continents.

Land bridge
Siberia
Alaska

The Rise of the Aztecs

The beginnings of the Aztec nation were humble. Yet in the space of a few hundred years, it rose to rule over most of Mexico. Also known as the Mexica or Tenochca, the Aztecs arrived in the Valley of Mexico in the 13th century after a long journey. They were the last of many tribes to settle in the area and the best land had already been taken. Life was miserable as they were forced to work as slaves for the more powerful tribes.

Aztec beginnings

The Aztecs came from Aztlán (Place of Herons) in the west of Mexico. In 1325, they set up home on an uninhabited island on the western edge of Lake Texcoco in the Valley of Mexico. They settled where they saw the sign of an eagle as promised by their gods. Today, this symbol appears in the middle of the Mexican flag (top).

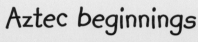

Aztec manuscripts had footprints showing their migration route.

The Toltec influence

The Aztecs greatly admired the warlike Toltecs, who dominated most of central Mexico between AD 900 and 1170. Tula, the Toltec capital, was located just north of the Valley of Mexico. The main temple at Tula had stone columns carved into warriors and plumed serpents (right). The Aztecs called this period the golden age and honoured Tula as a centre of power and civilisation.

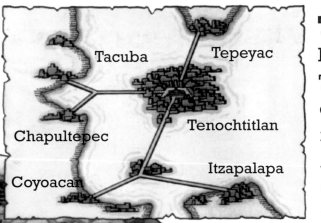

The glorious city

From a few reed and grass huts, Tenochtitlan grew into one of the largest cities in the world. It was linked to the mainland by three causeways (*left*). Access was controlled by wooden drawbridges. In the middle of the city were two large shrines dedicated to the gods – Huitzilopochtli (god of war and the Sun) and Tlaloc (god of rain and green growth). In 1519, Tenochtitlan had nearly 300,000 inhabitants.

The water's edge

Tenochtitlan was situated on a lake and its streets were canals. People got around by boat and lived in one-storey homes made out of sticks and mud bricks, with thatched roofs.

Chinampas

To make the most of their swampy land, the Aztecs dug large ditches and canals. They also built chinampas or 'rafts' made from branches. On these floating platforms the Aztecs grew their plant foods.

The Aztec Empire

Just as Tenochtitlan grew into a large city, so the Aztec Empire expanded by fighting wars. In 1428, following a victorious battle, the Triple Alliance was formed between Tenochtitlan and the neighbouring towns of Texcoco and Tacuba. During the reign of Moctezuma I (1440-68) and his successor, Axayacatl (1468-81), the Aztec Empire continued to spread.

Gulf of Mexico

Aztec Empire

Tenochtitlan

Pacific Ocean

Warfare
War was basic to the Aztec way of life. The warriors wore very elaborate costumes.

War and empire

War was regarded as the most glorious of all Aztec activities. Not only did it extend their territory, but it also gave them captives for sacrifice. By the time of the Spanish Conquest in 1519, the Aztecs ruled most of Mexico. The land was divided up into states, and the inhabitants were forced to pay tribute to the ruling Aztecs.

Jaguar Knights
Jaguar Knights (*above*) wore jaguar skins and were seen as the soldiers of the night sky.

Eagle Knights

A man's status depended on his success as a warrior. Very successful fighters were allowed to enter an order like the Knights of the Eagle (*below*). They got to wear elaborate helmets and quilted cotton body armour.

Weaponry

The Aztec warrior was trained to use a range of weapons. These included bows and arrows, spears and wooden sword-clubs edged with a hard volcanic glass called obsidian. They used the atlatl or spearthrower (*below*) to propel barbed darts or javelins.

Tribute

The great city of Tenochtitlan grew too large to support itself and had to rely on payments of tribute, such as costumes and shields, from towns the Aztec warriors had conquered. To keep a record of what each town provided, lists were made in picture form (*left*). The towns are shown here by pictures in the left-hand column.

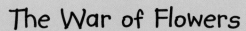

The War of Flowers

To keep their gods happy, the Aztecs believed they had to offer a never-ending supply of human sacrifices. These captives came from wars against the Tlaxcalans. The combats became known as the xochiyaoyotl, or 'flowery war'.

Aztec Religion

The Aztecs believed they were 'the people of the Sun'. Huitzilopochtli (hummingbird-on-the-left) was the god of war and the Sun, and was the Aztecs' most important god. They worshipped many gods including Tezcatlipoca (smoking mirror) and Quetzalcoatl (plumed serpent, above). The Aztecs also believed that to help the Sun on its daily journey across the sky, they had to offer a constant stream of human sacrifices.

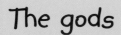

The gods

Aztecs pictured their gods using gold, jade, stone, clay, wood and other materials. The emblem of Tezcatlipoca was made from a human skull and decorated with mosaic pieces of turquoise, lignite and shell. Mictlantecuhtli, Lord of the Region of Death, is shown here with a death mask.

Tezcatlipoca

Mictlantecuhtli

Human sacrifice

Human sacrifice was practised by the Aztecs on a huge scale. Their victims had their hearts cut out with a very ornate sacrificial knife.

Temples

The Aztec city was dominated by an enormous double temple of Huitzilopochtli and Tlaloc (*right*). In 1487, to mark its opening, 20,000 captive warriors were sacrificed to the gods.

Time and the cosmos

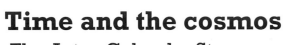

The Aztec Calendar Stone (*right*) marks the five world-creations. They used a solar calendar of 365 days and a sacred calendar of 260 days, the combination of which led to a cycle of 52 years. Each year had many festivals like the Flying Dance. Five men climbed a pole, and while one played music the other four 'flew' to the ground suspended on ropes.

Pyramids

Egyptian pyramids were enormous tombs built out of stone. They covered a burial chamber and were thought to guarantee the well-being of kings in the afterlife. Early pyramids had stepped sides (*bottom*), but later ones were given straight sides to represent the Sun's rays. The Mayan peoples of ancient Mexico built pyramids with a temple on the top. Unlike the Egyptian pyramids, those in the New World were rarely used as tombs (*right*).

Aztec Society

Technochtitlan was divided into four sections and then divided again into wards known as calpulli. Each ward had its own temple and an elected head. The Aztec people had to live by strict laws. At the top of the heirarchy was the emperor and below him were the warriors, state officials and priests. Merchants and craft workers formed separate classes. Below these came the majority of the citizens, the slaves being the lowest order.

Everyday life

Life for the common people was strictly regulated, even down to what they wore. Women wore a wrap-around skirt and a tunic-like blouse. Men wore a loincloth with a short cape. If the cape came to the ankles, the punishment was death. Boys learned how to fish, tend the land and manage boats. Girls were taught how to spin cotton, weave clothing and prepare food.

Food

We eat many of the same foods as the Aztecs. They used maize for pancakes (known today as tortillas), and grew beans, squash, chilli peppers, avocado pears, sweet potatoes, tomatoes and cocoa. Animals eaten by the Aztecs included turkey.

Markets

The magnificent markets of the Aztec capital sold food, obsidian blades, ornaments, jade, feathers, pottery and textiles. Cocoa beans or lengths of cloth could be used as currency. Bartering was commonplace, offering other goods or services in exchange. Gold dust was another method of payment and it was carried in a hollowed-out feather quill.

The emperor

At the top of the Aztec hierarchy was the emperor. Theoretically appointed by the gods, in reality the emperors were elected by a group of high-ranking officials, priests and warriors. The emperor lived in splendour, with magnificent palaces and gardens in different places. He would reward brave warriors with gifts such as jewels and feather ornaments (*left*). The emperor was carried around in a litter by four chiefs (*main picture*).

Merchants and trade

The state relied heavily on trade, and Aztec merchants were a powerful and privileged class. Their missions along a network of trade routes could take many months, returning with luxury goods. Sometimes they acted as spies, travelling in disguise into enemy territory. Although many were rich, they had to keep it a secret in public, by law.

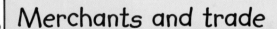

The Arts

Aztec men and women wove their own clothes and made their own pots. There were also professional craftworkers who lived in special areas of the city. Goldsmiths, feather-workers and jewellers were called 'Toltecs'. Painters were also considered to be special. Some decorated monuments with brightly coloured wall-paintings, while others worked as scribes, creating manuscripts called codices.

Gold!

Gold-working was a special craft introduced by the Mixtec craftsmen from Oaxaca. Gold was panned from local riverbeds and then made into ornaments. These included masks, animals, earrings, chest ornaments and armbands (*right*). Some specimens still survive today.

Language and song

The Aztecs spoke Nahuatl, which became the main tongue in central Mexico. Characters in the codices were often depicted with a blue speech-scroll to signify authority. Aztec songs were written by princes and priests.

14

Codices

In Aztec Mexico, codices were painted on folded strips of deerskin, bark paper, or even agave paper (*right*). They showed Aztec astrology, history, prophecy and tribute lists, all in picture form.

Feather-working

Among the most skilled workers were the amanteca, or feather-workers, who lived in a city ward called Amantla. They made headdresses and shields which were used by the high-ranking warriors. They also pasted feathers onto cloth or paper to make a dazzling mosaic. Some of the feathers used came from the vibrantly coloured quetzal bird. They were trimmed with gold, silver and gemstones.

Hieroglyphics

The ancient Egyptians wrote on papyrus paper, as well as carving inscriptions on stone (*below*). Like the Aztecs, they used a form of picture writing called hieroglyphics. This system used a combination of signs for ideas and sounds. By 1519, these symbols conveyed whole words. As an example, a scribe would use a footprint to show travel.

The Rise of the Incas

The Inca dynasty was founded around AD 1200 by Manco Capac at Cuzco in the Peruvian Andes. Capac and his descendents fought many battles to extend their territory. The first emperor to do this was Pachacuti (1438-71). He was followed by Topa Inca (1471-93) and Huayna Capac (1493-1525). At the end of Huayna Capac's reign, the Incas controlled an area 320 km (200 miles) wide and 3,520 km (2,200 miles) long.

Roads

A complex network of roads and bridges (*right*) linked all of the empire. Longest was the Andean road, which ran through the mountains. Messages from the regions were carried by runners to Cuzco.

Peoples of the Inca Empire

For more than 1,000 years, different peoples have inhabited the region that stretches from the Andean valleys to the Pacific. The powerful Chimú kingdom was one of the areas absorbed into the Inca Empire.

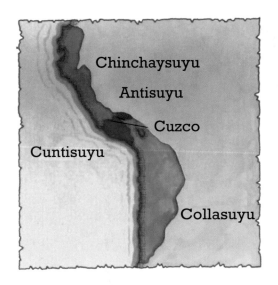

The four quarters

By 1525, the Empire stretched from Ecuador to Chile. It was known as the 'Land of Four Quarters' or Tahuantinsuyu: Chinchaysuyu in the north-west, Antisuyu in the north-east, Cuntisuyu in the south-west and Collasuyu in the south-east. Cuzco (meaning 'navel') was at its centre.

The Inca territories were so vast they included all types of climate and landscape. The coastal region is a narrow ribbon of desert where rain hardly ever falls. From here, the Andes

rise steeply to a high plateau that is broken by deep valleys which offer good arable land. To the east of the mountains lies the vast jungle of the Amazon river basin.

The emperor

The Sapa Inca ('Supreme Inca') was worshipped as the 'Son of the Sun'. Each Inca ruler built his own palace (*left*) in the centre of Cuzco. It was richly decorated, with walls adorned with gold and silver and hung with textiles.

The Nazca lines

The landscape of the Inca Empire was filled with the relics of the people who used to live there. Perhaps the most mysterious are the famous Nazca 'lines', which form vast figures in the desert. The designs include triangles, rectangles, spirals and even some animal

and bird forms. It is believed these lines could have some astronomical significance, or were created by cults linked with the sea, sky and mountains.

The Inca Empire

To keep the empire running smoothly, the Incas needed a highly organised system. New territories were ruled by Inca-trained officials from newly built towns. They taught people to obey Inca laws and to worship the Sun. The basic unit of the social structure was the ayllu, a farming community based on the family. From the top to the bottom of the social hierachy, everyone had a role to play. Anyone who failed in their duties had to face harsh penalties.

The social hierarchy

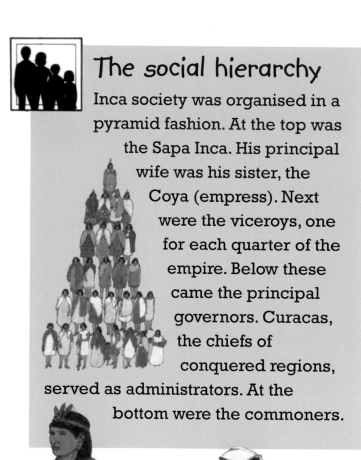

Inca society was organised in a pyramid fashion. At the top was the Sapa Inca. His principal wife was his sister, the Coya (empress). Next were the viceroys, one for each quarter of the empire. Below these came the principal governors. Curacas, the chiefs of conquered regions, served as administrators. At the bottom were the commoners.

Building for earthquakes

The west coast of North, Central and South America is constantly threatened by earthquakes. These are due to the massive plates that make up the Earth's crust rubbing against each

other. Cuzco and other Inca cities were built to withstand earthquakes. Inca stonemakers were so skilled they could build walls that bore being shaken by even the most powerful Earth tremors.

Clothing

Clothing indicated the social status and where the person came from. Garments were usually simple, but the elite's were brightly coloured. The Sapa Inca wore a braid, wound around the head, called a llauta.

Town planning

The Incas probably learned their planning skills from the Chimú. Around Cuzco's central plaza (the Holy Place) stood the palaces of the former and current Sapa Incas. The Sun Temple was nearby. The rest of the city was divided into four separate parts. Visitors had to stay in the quarter that corresponded with their province.

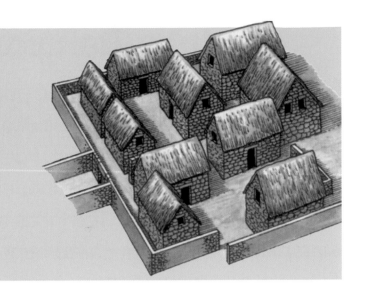

Conquered territories

When the Inca army conquered a new territory, their success was recorded on the quipu. One part of all fertile land was assigned to the Sun, a second share went to the emperor. What was left was divided up among the ayllus.

Quipu

The quipu is a system of knotted cords used by the Incas to store important information. Numbers and other data were indicated by knots of different sizes and positions on the strings. Quipus were tied and 'read' by special officials. It meant they could keep records of population, goods, herds and weapons.

Inca Religion

Religion kept the people of the Inca Empire united. At its heart was the cult of Inti, the Sun. Other important gods were Mamaquilla (the Moon), Pachamama (Mother Earth), Mamacocha (Mother Water) and Illapa (Thunder). These gods all represented Viracocha, the Creator. The Incas also worshipped holy sites, called huacas.

The Inca calendar

By using the Sun, Moon and stars, the Incas established a solar calendar of twelve months. Depending on the Sun's position in the sky, it was marked by special stones.

The Sapa Inca

To assert his power, each ruler claimed to be a son of the Sun. As the Sun ruled the skies, the Supreme Inca ruled the Earth. When the Sapa Incas died, their bodies were mummified and consulted as oracles.

Ceremony and sacrifice

The priests (*right*) held important positions in Inca society. They received one third of everything and both llamas and guinea pigs formed part of this 'taxation'. Perfect specimens were offered as sacrifices to ensure a good harvest. Sacrifices were also made to the Sun as it rose each day over the city of Cuzco.

The cult of the Sun

Inti, the Sun, was worshipped as the 'giver of life'. Temples were built for Inti all over the empire. At Cuzco's main temple the Incas kept gold images of the Sun (*left*). Herds and produce were used in rituals and as offerings. Inti Raimi, the Feast of the Sun, was celebrated in June.

Egyptian Sun worship

Long before the Incas, in ancient Egypt (c.2666-1640 BC), the supreme god was Ra, the Sun God (*below*). His symbols were the pyramid and the obelisk, and he was shown sailing the heavens in

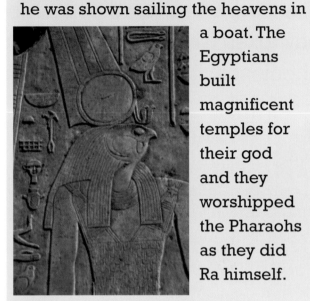

a boat. The Egyptians built magnificent temples for their god and they worshipped the Pharaohs as they did Ra himself.

Mummification

The Incas worshipped the remains of their ancestors. After the death of each emperor, his insides were removed and buried, but his body was preserved. It was dressed in fine fabrics and surrounded by precious objects. The bodies stayed in the palaces they had lived in. The Egyptians also mummified their dead and the South American Paracas people placed their mummies in deep caves.

Inca Society

Most commoners lived in farming and pastoral communities. Land and herds were divided into three parts. The first part belonged to the cult of the Sun. The second belonged to the Sapa Inca, his family and servants. The third was shared by members of the ayllu. Commoners had to pay taxes which were controlled by inspectors. In return for total obedience, the commoners were guaranteed lifelong security.

Housing

Other peoples, like the Chanca and the Colla, liked to live in round houses, but the Inca lived in rectangular ones. They were often built from stone with a thatched roof. They had very little

furniture and possessions and each house was checked regularly by inspectors.

Farming

Farmers used hoes, digging sticks and foot ploughs with a point of hard wood or bronze.
They practised two systems of agriculture. At high altitudes, people tended herds of llama and alpaca and also grew quinoa (a cereal) and potatoes. Maize was grown in the warm valleys and on low-lying, well-irrigated slopes. On the hotter lowland they grew cotton, tomatoes, squashes, chilli peppers, beans, peanuts, honey and fruits.

Animals

Crucial to the Andean way of life were the llama, alpaca, vicuña and guanaco, known collectively as cameloids. In the highland pastures of Peru and Bolivia, herds of llama and alpaca were kept as pack animals and also for wool. The guanaco and vicuña were allowed to roam freely. The guinea pig was kept by most households as a regular source of meat.

Taxation

Taxation was paid in the form of forced labour, or mit'a. Men were required to work on building roads, mining and the construction of buildings. Women had to weave cloth, while children and elderly people had to do light work. Food and goods were kept in state storehouses for times of hardship.

Reed boats

Inca people who lived near water used bundles of dried reeds to make lightweight boats.

Terracing is still used in many parts of the world, such as Indonesia. It is used on steep hillsides where normal agriculture would be impossible. It increases the area of land available and also prevents erosion of the soil.

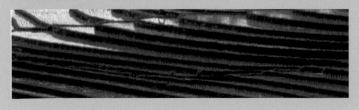

Arts and Sciences

Luxury goods were made by specialists who lived in the cities and were not subject to the normal taxes. They included metalsmiths, jewellers and experts in weaving. The Incas were also very good stonemasons and although their architecture was basic, it was solid. Huge granite blocks fitted together so closely they did not need mortar.

Jewellery

Inca jewellers were extremely skilled and made ornaments from a variety of gemstones and rare materials. Jewellery often indicated the social rank of a person. Shown

here is a pair of large earspools worn by the Incas.

Music

Music was played at the Inca court and during important ceremonies. Incas played cane flutes called quena, panpipes and drums. In war, conch shell trumpets and bone flutes were used.

Textiles

Women spun and wove to provide cloth for their families. Luxury cloth was made by specialist male weavers. These items were often decorated with gold and silver ornaments.

Arts and crafts

Professional artisans worked full time for the emperor, members of the elite and religious sects. Fine pottery vessels were made in a variety of shapes. Gold and silver were reserved for the luxury and ceremonial items. Gold was the symbolic colour of the Sun and also the Sapa Inca, while silver represented the Moon and the Coya (his wife).

Inca pottery vessel

Chimú hand of gold

Machu Picchu

Macchu Picchu is the best preserved of all the Inca towns (*main picture*). It lay forgotten until its rediscovery in 1911 by Hiram Bingham, the North American explorer. It is situated high in the Andes, and is a natural fortress protected by steep slopes.

Animal breeding

By 2000 BC, the Andean peoples had domesticated the llama (below) and alpaca. They were bred for sacrifice, their wool and also used as pack animals.

Weaving

Weavers used cotton and wool from their llama or alpaca herds, as well as the wild vicuña and guanaco. Textiles were made on the backstrap loom (*left*). This method is still used today and requires the warp threads to be stretched between two bars.

The Spanish Conquest

In 1532, when the Spanish Army reached the coast of Peru, Atahuallpa and Huascar, the sons of Huayna Capac, were arguing over succession. Francisco Pizarro was able to conquer the Inca Empire easily with just 63 horsemen and 200 foot soldiers. Most of the empire became the Viceroyalty of Peru and stayed so until 1824. In Mexico, Hernán Cortés began his conquest in 1519. By 1521, the capital of the Aztecs was in ruins and their empire was destroyed.

El Dorado

'El Dorado' means 'the Golden Man', and was the name given to a legendary chief who anointed himself with gold dust. Later imagined as a place, El Dorado became many sites including a volcanic lake.

Disease

Weakened by overwork in mines and on plantations, many Amerindians fell to epidemics such as smallpox. This spread of diseases was far more devastating than the bubonic plague in Europe in the 1300s.

Cortés

Hernán Cortés (1485-1547) landed in Mexico with about 600 men armed with weapons, gunpowder and horses. They were helped by the Tlaxcalans who were eager to be free of Aztec oppression, and quickly overcame Moctezuma II and his Aztec Army.

Felipe Guamán Poma de Ayala

Felipe Guamán Poma de Ayala wrote a manuscript of 1,188 pages, including 398 drawings. His work explores all the aspects of Inca history and religion, and gives detailed accounts of events and customs that took place in the Inca Empire.

Torture and brutality

The native South Americans were no match for the Spaniards, armed with gunpowder and weapons. Once in control, Spanish rule was marked by acts of cruelty. Many villages were burnt and their chiefs murdered.

The Catholic Church

In their desire to banish pagan beliefs, the Spanish destroyed many idols and burned codices. Using stones from pyramids and temples, they built their own churches and cathedrals.

Pizarro

Francisco Pizarro (c.1475–1541) started the conquest of Peru in 1532. The Inca Empire was already weakened by civil war and Pizarro used this to his advantage. He captured Atahuallpa, who tried to regain his freedom by filling his prison with gold. After a mock trial, the Inca was put to death. Pizarro himself was later killed by fellow Spaniards in another battle for leadership.

The Modern World

In Peru, the ancient language Quechua is still used today by many people. In Mexico, the descendants of the Aztecs, now called the Nahua, number over 1.4 million people. Most speak Spanish, but some speak only Nahuatl. The Nahua no longer build pyramids, but they still weave textiles and celebrate many of the same festivals.

Peruvian Amerindians (*below*)

Diego Rivera

The Mexican artist, Diego Rivera (1886-1957) was influenced by the brightly coloured codices and paintings of the ancient peoples. On the walls of buildings, he painted scenes from Aztec life (*below*).

Food and drugs

Diets changed with the introduction of New World foodstuffs such as potatoes, tomatoes, avocados, vanilla and turkeys. Xocoatl (pronounced 'chocoatl') was the Nahuatl word for chocolate. Maize was once central to Aztec and Inca survival. The Andeans traditionally chewed coca leaves to numb the effects of cold and hunger. Today, coca is used to make cocaine.

Archaeology

As archaeologists uncover more ruins, they give us detailed information about old civilisations. Gradually the original Inca structures are being uncovered. In the heart of Mexico City, for example, excavations are revealing the sacred precinct of the Aztecs (*right*). In Cuzco, they found the monastery of Santo Domingo which stands on the walls of the Coricancha, or Sun Temple.

Peru

Modern Peru has approximately 20 million people. Nearly half are Amerindians, descendants of the country's original inhabitants. Many tourists are drawn each year by the ruins of the Inca civilisation.

Mexico

Almost 300 years after the collapse of the Aztec Empire, the descendants of Spanish settlers won independence from Spain. In memory of the Aztecs (Mexica), the country was renamed Mexico. Today, the population exceeds 90 million people.

Mexico City

Mexico City is one of the largest cities in the world, and it is built on the ruins of Aztec Tenochtitlan. It has a complex drainage system to stop it from sinking into the ancient lake-bed. Steel and reinforced concrete help the tall buildings withstand the constant earthquakes.

INCAS:

c.1200 Cuzco founded by the legendary Manco Capac, first Sapa Inca.

1450 Pachacuti, the 9th Sapa Inca, enlarges the Inca Empire.

1498 Huayna Capac, the 11th Sapa Inca, extends conquest into Colombia.

1527 Francisco Pizarro makes first landing. Death of Huayna Capac is followed by civil war.

1532 Francisco Pizarro captures the Inca emperor Atahuallpa.

1533 Atahuallpa is executed by the Spanish.

1535 Collapse of the Inca Empire.

AZTECS:

1325 The Aztecs settle at Technochtitlan.

1440–68 Reign of Moctezuma I, father of the Aztec Empire.

1486–1502 Extension of the empire

1502–20 Reign of Moctezuma II and consolidation of the empire.

1519 Arrival of Hernán Cortés and his soldiers.

1521 Tenochtitlan destroyed by Spanish soldiers after a long siege.

1525 Collapse of the Aztec Empire.

8000 BC

First hieroglyphs (picture writing) in Egypt c.3500 BC

Old Kingdom in Egypt 2686–2150 BC

Pyramids built in Egypt during Old Kingdom

Egyptian Middle Kingdom 2040–1640 BC

2000 BC

Tutankhamun – the boy pharoah 1347–1339 BC

New Kingdom in Egypt 1552–1085 BC

Romulus and Remus found the city of Rome 753 BC

500 BC Roman Empire c.27 BC–c.AD 476

Julius Caesar murdered 44 BC

Fall of the Roman Empire AD 476

Viking raids on Britain and France AD 793–1000

AD 1000 First Crusade to recapture Holy Land from Muslims AD 1096

First mechanical clock developed AD 1386

AD c.1200–1532 The Inca Empire in South America

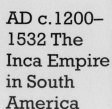

The Aztec Empire in Central America AD 1300s–1521

8000–5650 BC First cities – Jericho and Catal Hüyük

3500–3000 BC Wheel invented by the Sumerians

Rise of the Indus Valley civilisation 2500–1700 BC

Early Minoan period in Crete begins c.2500 BC

Stonehenge completed in England c.1500 BC

The destruction of Knossos in Crete. End of the Minoan period c.1400 BC

c.1766–1122 BC Shang Dynasty in China

Birth of Confucius 551 BC

c.500 BC Life of Guatama the Buddha

The Golden Age of Greece 479–431 BC

Alexander the Great conquers Persia, Syria and Egypt 333–330 BC

The Qin Dynasty in China 221–206 BC

The Great Wall of China completed in 214 BC

Samurai warriors of Japan AD 1100s–1850

The Plague, or Black Death, spreads in Europe AD 1300s

First mechanical printing press developed by Gutenberg in Germany in AD 1450

Christopher Columbus sets sail for the West Indies and becomes the first European to discover America AD 1492

Glossary

Acllas Young girls who lived in convents and were taught religious duties by the Mamacunas.

Adobe Unfired mud-brick.

Ayllu Traditional family or community group.

Cameloid Belonging to the Camelidae family – llama, alpaca, wild guanaco and vicuña.

Codex Pictorial manuscripts.

Curaca Ex-chief from subdued region of the Inca Empire.

Huaca Places or objects regarded as holy by the Inca peoples.

Mamacunas Consecrated or Chosen Women who lived in convents and served the Inca religion.

Mit'a Public-works tax paid by Inca subjects.

Nahuatl Language of the Aztecs.

Quechua Language of the Incas.

Quetzal Bird with long green tail feathers and coloured plumage.

Quipu Knotted cords used by the Incas for recording information.

Tahuantinsuyu Inca Empire – 'Land of the four Quarters'. At its centre was Cuzco.

Index

Photographic credits:

Abbreviations: t=top, m=middle, b=bottom, r=right, l=left

Cover, 3t, 12, 15t, 22t, 28t & b: Roger Vlitos; 2t, 3m & b, 4b, 20t, 23, 24t, ml, bl &br, 28m: Frank Spooner Pictures; 2m, 5, 17, 20b, 22b, 24mr, 25, 29b: Trip; 2b, 21b, 26t, 27tl & tr: South American Pictures; 4t, 15b, 16, 21t: Eye Ubiquitous; 7, 8, 14, 27b, 28–29, 29t: Mexicolore; 11t, 26b; Mary Evans Picture Library; 11m & b; Jenny Gosnold; 27m: Solution Pictures.